Purposeful Dating

PURPOSEFUL DATING

Training Program for Christians

- Study Guide -

Karen Maloy, Ed.S.

Mutual Blessings Books
Huntsville, AL
MBSuccess@karenmaloy.org
www.karenmaloy.org

Purposeful Dating

No part of this book may be reproduced or transmitted in any form or by any means electronically or mechanically, including photocopying and recording, or by any information storage or retrieval system, except as may be expressly permitted in writing by the publisher. Requests for permission should be addressed in writing to: MB Success Strategies at MBSuccess@karenmaloy.org. To order additional copies of this resource: write MB Success Strategies at MBSuccess@karenmaloy.org; call orders at (315) 657-3648 or order online at www.karenmaloy.org.

Printed in the United States of America

Unless otherwise indicated, all Scripture quotations are taken from the New International Version of the Bible.
The Purposeful Dating Training Program for Christians
Mutual Blessings Books
Publisher/Editor: MB Success Strategies
Published by Mutual Blessings - Huntsville, AL 35816
1-315-657-3648 - Website: **www.karenmaloy.org**

Printed in the United States of America. All rights reserved under International Copyright Law. Contents and/or cover may not be reproduced in whole or in part in any form without the express written consent of the publisher.

Copyright © 2013 Karen Maloy

All rights reserved.

ISBN-13: 978-0985660864

Purposeful Dating

CONTENTS

	Introduction	3
1	Covenant	6
2	Pre-Evaluations	11
3	The Real Cause of Poor Relationship Habits	16
4	Definition, Purpose and Result	26
5	Identifying the Problem	34
6	What You Need to Know	40
7	Principles to Guide You	50
8	Final Thoughts	67
9	Follow-Up	73

Purposeful Dating

HOW TO USE THIS PROGRAM

The Purposeful Dating Program is to help you understand and manage yourself more effectively while you are building your relationships. Ultimately, it is a comprehensive program for change. Change in your dating behavior. Change for the better in in your relationships. Each lesson in the program builds on the one before. It is important to start at the beginning and proceed through the program according to instructions.

What To Do First

Watch the Purposeful Dating Program Start DVD.

1. Before you do anything else, watch the Starting Line DVD. Karen will give you important information that will help you to change your behavior faster and more effectively. I will explain how the program works, what to do, and what to expect as you begin using these tools for changing your thinking. Watch this DVD before you begin the audio lessons.
2. Go to the workbook. Read all the information in the introduction.
3. Take the Self-Assessment, which his found on page 5 of the workbook at the end of the introduction.
4. After you have listened to Audio Lesson One, read the information in Workbook Session One. Then answer the

Training Program for Christians

questions Karen provides for you at the end of the lesson. The questions are specific directions to help you to explore your views, and apply the information you have just learned to your own situation. It's a good idea to listen to the audio lessons again one or two days after you first review it, or at any time if you are feeling challenged or unsure, in order to help reinforce the new ideas you will be learning.

The program will continue in this sequence –

- ➢ Audio Lessons
- ➢ Workbook Questions
- ➢ Action Steps Development to practice and reinforce the new information learned

What to Expect When Implementing This program

Take your time. You did not become this way overnight, so at least allow yourself ample time to make adjustments. Since you are simply reflecting upon characteristics in this lesson, do not expect to accomplish much beyond that in this lesson. Continue to use this strategy to identify any behaviors that you become aware throughout this workbook. Write those behaviors down in a notebook, and you will be able to come back and address them at a later date.

Purposeful Dating

ONE STEP AT A TIME

I recommend completing only one section a week. You will not be able to absorb all of the information if you rush through this program. Although it is suggested that you complete all sections in this workbook, please feel free to skip over those things which you have demonstrated proficiency in. However, keep in mind that some skills build upon another, and it may be necessary for you to repeat.

Complete the lessons in order and do one each week.

You will be applying new information based upon your own skills.. As you do, you will find the week-by-week approach is the quickest and most effective way to transform you behavior and improve your learning experience.

Important Note to Participants:

The Purposeful Dating Program provides participants with tools and techniques designed to help them to become more efficient. It is not designed to deal with individuals who have learning, mental or emotional disorders, and the strategies will not work for all types of individuals at all stages of development. Various factors may affect whether the program is effective with a particular individuals, including age and developmental level, the learning setting/environment, and the implementation of the program.

Individuals who exhibit behaviors which are indicative of severe emotional or learning disabilities, should continue to receive additional assistance from a qualified professional. This program is not intended to take the place of professional treatments, and is not a substitute for professional assistance. It is an additional resource to assist you to improve as an individual.

All the statements in the Purposeful Dating Program represent the opinions of its author, Karen Maloy.

Listen to the Transform Your Life Starting Video

Training Program for Christians

COVENANT

1. *I admit that I have made some bad decisions and they have hindered my success.*
2. *I believe that within me is the power to recover my life.*
3. *I prayerfully ask God to forgive me for my past choices.*
4. *I make a decision to assume responsibility for my own life and to stop blaming others for my choices.*
5. *I choose to forgive all individuals who have wronged me in the past and the present, and to release them from all offenses whether real or imagined.*
6. *I commit to do a honest and complete inventory of my life - healthy and unhealthy.*
7. *I commit to addressing all discoveries and to remove all identified deficits.*
8. *I commit to looking at all of my relationships (past and present) to identify my responsibility in their condition*
9. *I commit to continue to take a personal inventory, and to set and follow through with all goals to change my current state in life.*
10. *I will seek to improve my relationship with God, others, and myself, and promptly admit when I am wrong.*

Signed:_____Date: _____

This course is a self-paced personal development program and does not offer or take the place of professional therapy.

Purposeful Dating

Welcome to the Purposeful Dating Program!

Struggling in relationships can cause individuals to feel isolated, frustrated and embarrassed. But those days can be over for you. You no longer have to feel that you are alone. I plan to be here with you every step of the way, providing personalized coaching and additional assistance to help you to take control of your own life.

The Purposeful Dating program is designed to help individuals to become more effective in dating by increasing knowledge and skill sets needed to be successful in the dating environment.

I believe that poor relationships are marked by a lack of understanding, poor relationship building skills, and an inability to control oneself. In my view, having feelings of anger, frustration, anxiety and depression are problems which have to be solved in ways that don't cause self-defeat which could further lead to poor dating experiences. In this program, I seek to give individuals the tools that they need to comprehend how they function, and to provide the tools they need to address the problems which arise in dating environments effectively. First I will address some of the words and language which I will use in this program.

Subjects in this program will be referred to with masculine pronouns as in "he" or "him" just for the sake of simplicity and consistency. In no way should it be implied that this would be useful

Training Program for Christians

for male students only. It is also important to note that this information is for females, and also younger participants if they are able to rationalize and critically analyze subject content.

Children and adolescents will sometimes be referred to as "youth" within this program. Due to the wide application of this material, I feel that the terms would be best summed up by utilizing the word "students" or "learners".

This workbook is intended as a guide to support your use of the Transform Your Dating program and is not a stand-alone product. It is important to follow the directions given to get the best results. As you work on change, choose only one thing at a time to work on given complete attention to understanding that skill, and then move onto the next one. The purpose of this is to give each individual the opportunity to determine what works best for them.

Congratulations on taking this important step towards transforming and taking control of your relationships. I'm going to give you lots of information that you can start using today and plenty of help to help you succeed. So let's get started.

Minister Karen Maloy, Ed.S.

Purposeful Dating

ABOUT KAREN MALOY

For almost three decades Karen Maloy has pursued education. In graduate school Karen majored in Adult Education specializing in Workplace Learning and Staff Development. She also obtained her Ed.S. in Education specializing in Teaching and Learning in May, 2011 from Liberty University. Karen has created an approach to dating which challenges individuals to take a proactive approach to their dating. The Purposeful Dating Christian Dating program will also encourage individuals to take control of their own relationship building abilities, and not rely on the skills of others.

Karen brings a wealth of personal experience into the arena of teaching and learning, and has a good reason to focus on this content, having experienced many unhealthy relationships in her life. Many of these strategies were not researched but personally discovered by her to help her to build better relationships.

Born in 1965, Karen began her collegiate career at the age of 15 after being labeled and as a gifted learner in the fourth grade. She was placed in the Metropolitan Achievement Program, and for the next four years attended classes with the same group of children in specialized accelerated learning courses. She was the given the opportunity to take her GED at the age of 15 and passed; however since the law states that a child cannot receive their GED until they are 16, it was mailed to her on her 16th birthday in 1982. She began college at Fulton-Montgomery Community College in 1981 under an early admissions program, and received her Associates degree in Humanities at the age of 17. Although she graduated with honors and made the dean's list all but one semester, but failed to develop her social skills which ordinarily occur in high school. Her academic career for the next eight years was even less successful. Attending three different universities, she finally dropped out of school having lost interest in education altogether. After more than fourteen years being away from school, she was given the opportunity to return to school during her workday so that she would not have to pay a babysitter for her to attend schools in the evening. This was important as she trying to raise four children as a single parent.

Training Program for Christians

Although Karen continued to excel academically as well as professionally, her previous relationship experiences continued to plague her and she continued to have unsuccessful relationships. She lacked self-confidence, self-love and self-esteem; and as a result, she continued to pursue relationships with individuals who had commitment issues, lacked intimacy, and who also had poor relationship building skills. It was many years before she realized that she was part of the problem, but when she did Karen also found her niche.

While pursuing her degree at Liberty University, Karen began her own business providing academic and life skills coaching. The focus of that work was to provide individuals with the tools to be successful, and others to take control of their lives by developing effective life, communication, and self-management skills.

Today, Karen Maloy continues to provides training and consultations to students in Christian dating, life skills, effective communication, as well as teach classes and conduct workshops for local ministries and schools. The Purposeful Dating program was developed to expand this message to a wider audience of individuals who are struggling in this area. This program offers individuals the same techniques Karen has used for herself and in her own coaching business.

PRE-EVALUATIONS

Training Program for Christians

PRE-EVALUATIONS

Once you have viewed the video and listened to the introduction, answer the questions in this Self-Assessment. This questionnaire will help you identify the behaviors which are essential for your progress in this area.

Directions: Evaluate yourself in each of these categories. Give yourself a score of (3) for always, (2) for sometimes, and (1) for never. When you are done total your score, and be prepared to reflect upon and defend your answers.

	Always	Sometimes	Never
I plan for my success.			
I learn from past mistakes.			
I know how to evaluate myself objectivity and honestly.			
I set goals for my life.			
I have good problem solving abilities.			
I am an active listener.			
I know what my strengths and weaknesses are.			
I use effective time management strategies			
I know how to manage distractions.			
I am always working to improve myself.			
I am well prepared for a relationship.			
I convey my thoughts and ideas clearly when communicating.			
I know how to manage my life, health and my finances.			
I am good at handling disappointments.			
I understand the importance of good decision-making.			

Purposeful Dating

Your Dream Dating Experience

Think about your perfect dating experience. What would it look like? Describe this dream experience.

_____

_____

_____

_____

_____

_____

_____

Which of the life skills are you going to need to work on?

_____

_____

_____

_____

_____

_____

_____

Training Program for Christians

List the skills that you have identified proficiency in? Pick three and describe situations that required you to use that skill.

_____

_____

_____

_____

_____

_____

_____

_____

_____

_____

_____

_____

_____

_____

_____

_____

_____

_____

_____

Purposeful Dating

List the skills that you have identified still need development? Pick three and describe situations that demonstrate your inability to apply that skill.

_____

_____

_____

_____

_____

_____

_____

_____

_____

_____

_____

_____

_____

_____

_____

_____

_____

_____

Training Program for Christians

The Real Causes of Poor Relationship Habits

Purposeful Dating

THE REAL CAUSES OF POOR RELATIONSHIP HABITS

The reasons given for inappropriate dating behaviors are generally unsatisfactory when compared to the scope of the behavior themselves. Inappropriate social responses can be best understood as actions triggered by the need to compensate for an endless variety of perceptions, thoughts, and feelings that the individuals knows that they are counterproductive, yet, they feel are beyond their control.

Poor relationships are not caused by the other individual

- Saying the wrong thing
- Doing the wrong thing
- Expecting too much
- Being unsympathetic
- Failing to understand
- Refusing to listen
- Failing to give enough of one's self or one's time to invest in them

Poor relationships habits compensates for the individual's

- Faulty reasoning
- Poorly developed relationship-building skills
- Perception of powerlessness
- Low tolerance for frustration
- Intellectual and functional laziness
- Fears and insecurities

Poor relationship habits are not

- A symptom of the internet or social media
- Caused by low self-esteem

Poor dating habits are:

- Practiced and reinforced although counterproductive
- Centered on the individual, and
- Are learned and rewarded behaviors

Training Program for Christians

Characteristics and Practice of Individuals with Poor Relationship Habits

If you step back to reflect upon your dating experiences, you will see that common themes or patterns often emerge. These patterns appear to be reactions to others in your life; however, they are in fact maladaptive learning practices that can be summarized in the following categories:

1) **Victim** – The learner view themselves as being in the role of the victim, and reject the idea that they are responsible for what happens, and that they should be held responsible.

2) **Unfair** – The learner views others as being unfair, thereby justifying his failure to apply himself. When challenged, he seeks to make unfairness the focus, instead of focusing on what he can do to change.

3) **Misunderstood** – The individual demands that everyone must try to understand and adapt to him, while he routinely refuses to understand and adapt to others.

4) **Wishful Thinkers** – While the learner may want to improve their relationships, self-reflection and evaluations are avoided, resisted, or rejected.

5) **Procrastinators** – The learner will procrastinate, repeatedly putting off any activity, task, or responsibility that interferes with what they want to do at that moment.

6) **Misinformed** – The learner becomes a master at telling others what they want to hear, and spend little time trying to understand the relationship.

7) **Blame Shifters** – The learner does not acknowledge that they are responsible. The issue is instead turned around to make the other individual feel responsible. "I did everything right but they just refused to change"; or "I know I made some mistakes, but I should at least get credit for that." It puts the other person in the position of having to defend their reaction to their shortcomings.

Purposeful Dating

8) **Incompleters** – The individual completes the part of the process which is the easiest, and expects to receive the full benefits of completion.

Training Program for Christians

CHARACTERISTICS PROFILE

Directions: Please review the following sets of characteristics or patterns of behavior. Consider how they match you, and identify which characteristics are the most problematic for you. Then, using a rating scale of 1-5 rate yourself against each of the characteristics. Use 1 if the characteristic is least like you, 2-4 which for those behaviors which you have seen that cause some problems, and 5 for those characteristics which are most like you and thus cause significant problems.

Victim

Do you...

_____ Blame others for not meeting responsibilities

_____ Blame others for inappropriate responses

_____ Always have an excuse ready to justify yourself

_____ Fight for your right to be a victim

_____ Resist efforts to appropriately solve the problem which is causing distress

_____ Want to focus on being a victim instead of taking responsibility for the original problem

Unfair

_____ View normal expectations as being unfair

_____ Refuse to follow "unfair" directions or meet "unfair" expectations

_____ Complain that consequences for inappropriate responses are unfair

Misunderstood

_____ Claim that you are different from others and that this is just the way that you are

_____ Demand to be understood

Purposeful Dating

____ Accuse others of not understanding you

____ Focus on the lack of understanding by others rather than the original problem.

Wishful Thinkers

____ Have an unrealistically high opinion of your skills and abilities

____ Talk about how you wish things were, while rejecting goals and commitments designed to meet those wishes

____ Act as if talking about making positive changes is the same as doing things to make positive changes

Procrastinators

____ Constantly put off activities, assignments, or tasks which you perceive as responsibilities

____ Respond unfavorably when pressured to do activities, assignments, or tasks in a timely fashion right then and there.

Misinformed

____ Deliberately omit or provide vague details to exert the least amount of effort

____ Pretend to have misunderstood when confronted about actions

____ Say yes without meaning it in order to avoid conflict

____ Act confused when challenged on some comment or behaviors

Blame Shifters

____ Put others on the defensive when you are clearly wrong

____ Put others on the defensive when you receive an unfavorable evaluation

____ Use statements such as "You weren't clear" or "I didn't understand", as a way to avoid dealing with the issue at hand or to receive leniency

Training Program for Christians

Incompleters

_____ Do incomplete jobs on assignments and responsibilities

_____ Expect full rewards for incomplete efforts

_____ Respond unfavorably when reminded of the full expectation of the responsibility

_____ React unfavorably when not given full credit for an assignment partially done.

Now review the ratings you have given these characteristics. Some characteristics may not describe you, while others will be accurate descriptions of you. If you have rated everything either very high or very low, go back and force yourself to be more discriminating, giving a range of scores from 1 to 5. This is where we will determine where to begin.

Even though it feels overwhelming, it is important to focus on those concerns which are the most problematic right now, to have the best chance for improvement. You can always go back later after mastery of the most problematic to work on other issues. While you may be tempted to work on everything at once, the smaller the focus in this lesson, the better your chances for success.

REFLECTION

Based on your self-assessment, please take a moment and explain what you have learned about yourself. Use more sheets if necessary.

_____

_____

_____

_____

_____

Purposeful Dating

Training Program for Christians

ACTION STEPS

A. Identify three characteristics you use to avoid taking responsibility for your own actions.

_____

_____

_____

_____

B. Identify three situations where you use the power of negative responses to get your way, avoid consequences, or escape responsibility.

_____

_____

_____

_____

_____

_____

_____

_____

Purposeful Dating

_____

_____

_____

_____

_____

C. When you find yourself using a negative behavior, declare to yourself that that behavior is not going to solve the problem. For example say "When I asked them to stop spending time with their friends because I felt uncomfortable when they were gone, it did not address the jealousy issue that I have. I understand that I am jealous because I am insecure, and I must address this problem if I want to have healthier relationships." Choosing one of the situations identified above, develop a declaration for yourself.

_____

_____

_____

_____

_____

The Definition, Purpose and Result of Dating

Purposeful Dating

Its Definition, Purpose and Result

Scripture Reflection:

Then God said, "Let us make mankind in our image, in our likeness, so that they may rule over the fish in the sea and the birds in the sky, over the livestock and all the wild animals,[a] and over all the creatures that move along the ground."
So God created mankind in his own image,
   in the image of God he created them;
   male and female he created them.
God blessed them and said to them, "Be fruitful and increase in number; fill the earth and subdue it. Rule over the fish in the sea and the birds in the sky and over every living creature that moves on the ground."
Genesis 1:26-28

Listen to Audio 2 - Definition, Purpose and Result

Training Program for Christians

What did you learn about yourself after listening to this section?

_____

_____

_____

_____

How does your idea of dating differ from God's plan for relationships?

_____

_____

_____

_____

How does your relationship with God influence your life decisions?

_____

_____

_____

_____

Purposeful Dating

Reflecting upon your past relationships, what have you been reproducing?

_____

_____

_____

_____

_____

How have you been impacted by your past relationships?

_____

_____

_____

_____

_____

What are some of the frustrations that you have faced concerning dating?

_____

_____

_____

_____

_____

Training Program for Christians

Now that you know that the end result of dating should be marriage, what have you been doing which has proven to be counterproductive to that outcome?

_____

_____

_____

Take a moment to evaluate each component of your worldview and explain why you have come to that conclusion.

Nature of God

_____

_____

_____

_____

_____

Nature of Man

_____

_____

_____

_____

Purposeful Dating

Your view of knowledge

_____

_____

_____

_____

Your view of right or wrong

_____

_____

_____

_____

Your view of the future

_____

_____

_____

_____

ACTION STEPS

A. Identify three characteristics you use which may encourage unhealthy relationship building.

_____

_____

Training Program for Christians

_____

_____

_____

B. Identify up to three situations where your dating habits may have hindered the development of you (or those you influence) spiritually or morally.

_____

_____

_____

_____

_____

_____

_____

_____

_____

_____

_____

_____

_____

Purposeful Dating

_____

_____

C. Choosing one of the situations identified above, develop a declaration for yourself.

_____

_____

_____

_____

Training Program for Christians

Identifying the Problem

Purposeful Dating

Identifying the Problem

Scripture Reflection

The thief comes only to steal and kill and destroy; I have come that they may have life, and have it to the full. John 10:10

Listen to Audio Section 2 - Identifying the Problem

What did you learn about yourself after listening to Section 2?

_____

_____

_____

_____

_____

Training Program for Christians

How is your idea of dating similar to "The Illusion"?

_____
_____
_____
_____
_____
_____

What does the idea of a "perfect mate" mean to you?

_____
_____
_____
_____
_____
_____

Reflecting upon your past relationships, what did you do to positive contribute to it?

_____
_____
_____
_____
_____

Purposeful Dating

What role did you play in its demise?

_____
_____
_____
_____
_____
_____

How has the enemy been instrumental in negatively impacting your identity?

_____
_____
_____
_____
_____

What does the term "sexual education" mean to you?

_____
_____
_____
_____

Training Program for Christians

Identify key people who have shaped your sexual education?

_____

_____

_____

_____

ACTION STEPS

A. Identify three characteristics you use which are counterproductive to healthy relationship building.

_____

_____

_____

_____

_____

B. Identify up to three situations where your dating habits may have hindered the development of you (or those you influence) spiritually or morally.

_____

_____

_____

_____

_____

Purposeful Dating

C. Choosing one of the situations identified above, develop a declaration for yourself.

Training Program for Christians

What You Need to Know

Purposeful Dating

What You Need To Know

Read and meditate on the following scriptures:

> *Train up a child in the way he should go; even when he is old he will not depart from it. Proverbs 22:6*
>
> *Do not withhold discipline from a child; if you strike him with a rod, he will not die. If you strike him with the rod, you will save his soul from Sheol. Proverbs 23:13-14*
>
> *Fathers, do not provoke your children to anger, but bring them up in the discipline and instruction of the Lord. Ephesians 6:4*
>
> *Whoever spares the rod hates his son, but he who loves him is diligent to discipline him. Proverbs 13:24*
>
> *The rod and reproof give wisdom, but a child left to himself brings shame to his mother. Proverbs 29:15*
>
> *Folly is bound up in the heart of a child, but the rod of discipline drives it far from him. Proverbs 22:15*
>
> *And if it is evil in your eyes to serve the Lord, choose this day whom you will serve, whether the gods your fathers served in the region*

Training Program for Christians

beyond the River, or the gods of the Amorites in whose land you dwell. But as for me and my house, we will serve the Lord." Joshua 24:15

My son, keep your father's commandment, and forsake not your mother's teaching. Bind them on your heart always; tie them around your neck. Proverbs 6:20-21

You shall teach them diligently to your children, and shall talk of them when you sit in your house, and when you walk by the way, and when you lie down, and when you rise. Deuteronomy 6:7

Fathers, do not provoke your children, lest they become discouraged. Colossians 3:2

After reading these scriptures, what does the term "mentor" mean to you?

_____

_____

_____

_____

_____

Listen to Audio Section 4- Parental and Individual Responsibility

What did you learn about yourself after listening to Section 3?

_____

_____

_____

_____

Purposeful Dating

Who have been the mentors in your life? How have they impacted you negatively? Positively?

_____
_____
_____
_____
_____

Reflecting upon the parental responsibility, answer the following questions.

How have your parents shaped your ideas about dating?

_____
_____
_____
_____
_____

What do you think is the relationship between parenting and dating?

_____
_____
_____
_____

Training Program for Christians

If you have children, what have you taught them about dating? If you don't, what will you teach them?

_____

_____

_____

_____

_____

Reflecting upon the individual responsibility, answer the following questions.

What are some of the misconceptions that you had about dating?

_____

_____

_____

_____

_____

Think about a time that you were disappointed in a past relationship. How did you handle it? What could you have done differently?

_____

_____

_____

_____

Purposeful Dating

Read Proverbs 31. What does it mean to you to be a Proverbs 31 mate?

_____

_____

_____

_____

_____

How would you describe your relationship health? Why?

_____

_____

_____

_____

_____

What are some of the things that you can do to prepare yourself for a healthy relationship?

_____

_____

_____

_____

Training Program for Christians

What are you looking for in a mate? Be specific.

_____

_____

_____

_____

_____

_____

Reflecting upon the good relationships in your life, identify what makes them good.

_____

_____

_____

_____

_____

_____

_____

_____

_____

_____

Purposeful Dating

What qualities, characteristics and skills do you have which would be beneficial in a relationship? Use additional sheets if necessary.

Training Program for Christians

ACTION STEPS

A. Identify three characteristics you display which indicate that you have been negatively impacted by previous relationships

_____

_____

_____

_____

B. Identify up to three situations where your negative emotions may have hindered your relationship.

_____

_____

_____

_____

_____

_____

_____

_____

Purposeful Dating

_____

_____

_____

_____

_____

C. Choosing one of the situations identified above, develop a declaration for yourself.

_____

_____

_____

_____

Training Program for Christians

Principles to Guide You

Purposeful Dating

Principles to Guide You

Scripture Reflection

> But mark this: There will be terrible times in the last days. ² People will be lovers of themselves, lovers of money, boastful, proud, abusive, disobedient to their parents, ungrateful, unholy, ³ without love, unforgiving, slanderous, without self-control, brutal, not lovers of the good, ⁴ treacherous, rash, conceited, lovers of pleasure rather than lovers of God— ⁵ having a form of godliness but denying its power. Have nothing to do with such people. 2 Timothy 3:3-5

Listen to Audio Section 4- Dating Rules

What did you learn about yourself after listening to Section 4?

_____

_____

_____

Training Program for Christians

Dating Rules

Now that you have been introduced to the dating rules, it is time to evaluate ourselves and to establish some guidelines for success. Taking a look at each dating rule, you are to identify what skills you need to develop so that you can ensure success in your dating experiences.

1. Understand the principle of being" evenly yoked"!

Read 2 Corinthians 6:14

What does it mean to be evenly yoked?

_____

_____

_____

_____

What areas of compatibility that you need in your relationships? (i.e. outdoorsman, sports, church attendance)

_____

_____

_____

_____

Purposeful Dating

2. Do not assume that age equates with maturity!

Read 1 Corinthians 13:11

What the term "maturity" mean to you? Be specific.

_____

_____

_____

_____

_____

How good are you at expressing your thoughts, feelings and ideas? *Give an example.*

_____

_____

_____

_____

_____

3. Your Relationship Will Not Complete You, Only Enhance You!

1 Corinthians 13:10

Identify your relationship needs. Your deficits.

_____

Training Program for Christians

What areas in your life are you expecting your potential mate to help you address?

    4.   *Understand the importance of balance in the body, soul, and spirit.*

Read Job 31:6

Describe what it means to have an intimate relationship with God?

Purposeful Dating

    5.   Understand what it means to be a Proverbs 31 Mate (male or female)

Read Proverbs 31

What is your understanding of what it means to be a godly mate?

_____

_____

_____

_____

_____

What areas do you need to improve upon?

_____

_____

_____

_____

    6.   Make sure that you are, and look for   signs that they are in touch with their own emotions.

Galatians 5:23

Describe what it means to be in touch with one's emotions?

_____

_____

Training Program for Christians

_____
_____
_____

What areas are you strong in? need help in?

_____
_____
_____
_____
_____

      7.   *Invest the time to study one another.*

Ephesians 4:29

What does the term "falling in love" mean to you?

_____
_____
_____
_____
_____

Why are the terms *commitment, time and effort* essential to relationships and dating?

_____

Purposeful Dating

___

How would you rate your communication skills? Why?

___

Give an example of a situation in which you believe that you used good communication skills.

___

Give an example of a situation where you believe you used poor communication skills.

___

Training Program for Christians

8. *Make sure that they know, understand and demonstrate godly love.*

1 Corinthians 13

What are the differences between godly and humanly love?

How does one demonstrate that they know how to love?

Purposeful Dating

How does one demonstrate that they love themselves?

_____

_____

_____

_____

9. *Pay attention to how they handle conflict and anger.*

Ephesians 4:26

What does the term "communication" mean to you? Why is it important?

_____

_____

_____

_____

_____

_____

What are some of the results of poor communication?

_____

_____

_____

Training Program for Christians

Why is it important that one knows how to handle conflict and confrontation?

10. Do not submit until they commit!

Read Ephesians 5:21-28

Describe your understanding of biblical submission.

How does submission differ from obedience?

Purposeful Dating

Why is it important that you wait for a commitment before you submit?

_____

_____

_____

_____

_____

ACTION STEPS

A. Identify three characteristics you use which are counterproductive to healthy relationship building.

_____

_____

_____

_____

B. Identify up to three situations where your dating habits may have hindered the development of you (or those you influence) spiritually or morally.

_____

_____

_____

Training Program for Christians

_____
_____
_____
_____
_____
_____
_____
_____
_____
_____

C. Choosing one of the situations identified above, develop a declaration for yourself.

_____
_____
_____

Purposeful Dating

Dangers of Choosing the Wrong Mate

The prudent see danger and take refuge,
  but the simple keep going and pay the penalty.
                                    Proverbs 22:3

But when he, the Spirit of truth, comes, he will guide you into all the truth. He will not speak on his own; he will speak only what he hears, and he will tell you what is yet to come. John 16:13

Listen to Audio - Final Thoughts

Share your thoughts after listening to this section. Use additional sheets if necessary.

_____

_____

_____

_____

_____

_____

What are some of the danger signs that you must look out for?

_____

_____

_____

_____

_____

Training Program for Christians

What does the idea of "commitment" mean to you?

_____

_____

_____

_____

_____

Reflecting upon your past relationships, identify what things made them a wrong mate? Be specific.

_____

_____

_____

_____

_____

_____

Reflecting upon your past relationships, identify what things made you a wrong mate? Be specific.

_____

_____

_____

_____

_____

Purposeful Dating

ACTION STEPS

A. Identify three characteristics you use which could potentially make you a wrong mate. Be specific.

_____

_____

_____

_____

_____

B. Identify up to three situations where you displayed characteristics which could potentially make you a wrong mate.

_____

_____

_____

_____

_____

_____

_____

Training Program for Christians

_____

_____

_____

_____

_____

_____

_____

C. Choosing one of the situations identified above, develop a declaration for yourself.

_____

_____

_____

_____

Final Thoughts

Purposeful Dating

Final Thoughts

How has your idea of dating changed after going through this program?

_____
_____
_____
_____
_____
_____

Now that you have completed this program, what does the idea of a "perfect mate" mean to you?

_____
_____
_____
_____
_____
_____

Reflecting upon your current relationships, identify one person who you would believe would make ideal mate?   Why?

_____
_____
_____
_____

Purposeful Dating

Reflecting upon your current relationships, identify one person who you believe would NOT make ideal mate? Why?

_____

_____

_____

_____

_____

_____

Personal Reflection

What aspect of Purposeful Dating was most meaningful for you?

_____

_____

_____

_____

_____

_____

_____

_____

Training Program for Christians

Has going through this programs changed any of the established beliefs and mindsets you already had? Identify. Use additional sheets if necessary.

_____

_____

_____

_____

_____

_____

_____

_____

_____

_____

Has it revealed any areas of difficulty and if so, what are they?

_____

_____

_____

_____

_____

Purposeful Dating

After reviewing your previous action plans, identify what changes you are going to implement in your life to ensure success in your future dating experiences? Use additional sheets if necessary.

_____

_____

_____

_____

_____

_____

_____

_____

_____

_____

_____

_____

_____

_____

_____

_____

Training Program for Christians

DECLARATION

Take a moment to review the declarations you wrote in the previous sections. The final step in this program is for you to write a declaration which will serve as a reminder of what you have learned about yourself, and your commitment to change wrong ideologies. Take a moment to write a commitment statement to your future success. i.e. "I am committing to implementing the changes necessary to ensure that I establish successful relationships. I am committed to ensuring that I glorify God in all my relationships, etc..."

_____

_____

_____

_____

_____

_____

_____

_____

_____

_____

_____

_____

_____

PROGRAM FOLLOW-UP

Training Program for Christians

PROGRAM FOLLOW-UP

Take a moment to review the Assessments you completed on pages 12-15. It is important that you address the areas that you have identified as areas you are not proficient in. After identifying those areas, identifying a plan of action following the same pattern.

Just as I suggested when you began this program, I encourage you to take it one step at a time. Resist the temptation to tackle all of these in the next few weeks. It has taken you a long time to become the person that you are today, and any changes will not occur overnight. You will not be able to develop new habits if you hurry through these steps. Give yourself time to apply the new action plans that you develop, and then allow yourself to master each before moving to the next life skill. The first one has been started for you.

LIFE SKILL

1. **I plan for success.**

ACTION PLAN

Identify 2 characteristics you intend to use which would prove proficiency in this area.

Identify Long-term and short-term goals

Create a timeline for completing those goals.

Identify a situation where you displayed characteristics which could hinder your development in this area

Purposeful Dating

<u>When I do not use a planner, I often forget what I have to get done until it is too late to get it done efficiently</u>

What can you do differently?

<u>I will write down what I want to do, and then look at my plan everyday to make sure that I do not forget.</u>

Develop a declaration for yourself.

_____

_____

_____

TRACK YOUR PROGRESS

_____

_____

_____

_____

_____

_____

_____

Training Program for Christians

2. _____

ACTION PLAN

Identify 2 characteristics you intend to use which would prove proficiency in this area.

_____

_____

Identify a situation where you displayed characteristics which could hinder your development in this area _____

_____

_____

What can you do differently? _____

_____

_____

_____

Develop a declaration for yourself.

_____

_____

_____

Purposeful Dating

TRACK YOUR PROGRESS

Training Program for Christians

3. _____

ACTION PLAN

Identify 2 characteristics you intend to use which would prove proficiency in this area.

_____

_____

Identify a situation where you displayed characteristics which could hinder your development in this area _____

_____

What can you do differently? _____

_____

_____

_____

Develop a declaration for yourself.

_____

_____

_____

Purposeful Dating

TRACK YOUR PROGRESS

_____
_____
_____
_____
_____
_____
_____
_____
_____
_____
_____
_____
_____
_____
_____
_____
_____

Training Program for Christians

4. _____

ACTION PLAN

Identify 2 characteristics you intend to use which would prove proficiency in this area.

_____

_____

Identify a situation where you displayed characteristics which could hinder your development in this area _____

_____

What can you do differently?_____

_____

_____

_____

Develop a declaration for yourself.

_____

_____

_____

Purposeful Dating

TRACK YOUR PROGRESS

Training Program for Christians

5. _____

ACTION PLAN

Identify 2 characteristics you intend to use which would prove proficiency in this area.

_____

_____

Identify a situation where you displayed characteristics which could hinder your development in this area _____

_____

What can you do differently?_____

_____

_____

_____

Develop a declaration for yourself.

_____

_____

_____

Purposeful Dating

TRACK YOUR PROGRESS

Training Program for Christians

6. _____

ACTION PLAN

Identify 2 characteristics you intend to use which would prove proficiency in this area.

_____

_____

Identify a situation where you displayed characteristics which could hinder your development in this area _____

_____

What can you do differently?_____

_____

_____

_____

Develop a declaration for yourself.

_____

_____

_____

Purposeful Dating

TRACK YOUR PROGRESS

_____

_____

_____

_____

_____

_____

_____

_____

_____

_____

_____

_____

_____

_____

Training Program for Christians

7. _____

ACTION PLAN

Identify 2 characteristics you intend to use which would prove proficiency in this area.

_____

_____

Identify a situation where you displayed characteristics which could hinder your development in this area _____

_____

What can you do differently?_____

_____

_____

_____

Develop a declaration for yourself.

_____

_____

_____

Purposeful Dating

TRACK YOUR PROGRESS

Training Program for Christians

8. _____

ACTION PLAN

Identify 2 characteristics you intend to use which would prove proficiency in this area.

_____

_____

Identify a situation where you displayed characteristics which could hinder your development in this area _____

_____

What can you do differently? _____

_____

_____

_____

Develop a declaration for yourself.

_____

_____

_____

Purposeful Dating

TRACK YOUR PROGRESS

Training Program for Christians

9. _____

ACTION PLAN

Identify 2 characteristics you intend to use which would prove proficiency in this area.

_____

_____

Identify a situation where you displayed characteristics which could hinder your development in this area _____

_____

What can you do differently?_____

_____

_____

_____

Develop a declaration for yourself.

_____

_____

_____

Purposeful Dating

TRACK YOUR PROGRESS

Training Program for Christians

10. _____

ACTION PLAN

Identify 2 characteristics you intend to use which would prove proficiency in this area.

_____

_____

Identify a situation where you displayed characteristics which could hinder your development in this area _____

_____

What can you do differently?_____

_____

_____

_____

Develop a declaration for yourself.

_____

_____

_____

Purposeful Dating

TRACK YOUR PROGRESS

Training Program for Christians

11. _____

ACTION PLAN

Identify 2 characteristics you intend to use which would prove proficiency in this area.

_____

_____

Identify a situation where you displayed characteristics which could hinder your development in this area _____

_____

What can you do differently?_____

_____

_____

_____

Develop a declaration for yourself.

_____

_____

_____

Purposeful Dating

TRACK YOUR PROGRESS

_____
_____
_____
_____
_____
_____
_____
_____
_____
_____
_____
_____
_____
_____
_____
_____
_____
_____

Training Program for Christians

12. _____

ACTION PLAN

Identify 2 characteristics you intend to use which would prove proficiency in this area.

_____

_____

Identify a situation where you displayed characteristics which could hinder your development in this area _____

_____

What can you do differently?_____

_____

_____

_____

Develop a declaration for yourself.

_____

_____

_____

Purposeful Dating

TRACK YOUR PROGRESS

Training Program for Christians

13. _____

ACTION PLAN

Identify 2 characteristics you intend to use which would prove proficiency in this area.

_____

_____

Identify a situation where you displayed characteristics which could hinder your development in this area _____

_____

What can you do differently?_____

_____

_____

_____

Develop a declaration for yourself.

_____

_____

_____

Purposeful Dating

TRACK YOUR PROGRESS

Training Program for Christians

14. _____

ACTION PLAN

Identify 2 characteristics you intend to use which would prove proficiency in this area.

_____

_____

Identify a situation where you displayed characteristics which could hinder your development in this area _____

_____

What can you do differently? _____

_____

_____

_____

Develop a declaration for yourself.

_____

_____

_____

Purposeful Dating

TRACK YOUR PROGRESS

Training Program for Christians

15. _____

ACTION PLAN

Identify 2 characteristics you intend to use which would prove proficiency in this area.

_____

_____

Identify a situation where you displayed characteristics which could hinder your development in this area _____

_____

What can you do differently?_____

_____

_____

_____

Develop a declaration for yourself.

_____

_____

_____

Purposeful Dating

TRACK YOUR PROGRESS

Training Program for Christians

To contact the author email @ MBSuccess@karenmaloy.org

Internet Address: www.karenmaloy.org

Your testimony or help received from this program when you write is greatly appreciated.

www.ingramcontent.com/pod-product-compliance
Lightning Source LLC
Chambersburg PA
CBHW070337230426
43663CB00011B/2355